SPRING
Clip Art A La Carte

Concept and compilation
by
Imogene Forte

Incentive Publications, Inc.
Nashville, Tennessee

For information about our audio products, write us at:
Newbridge Book Clubs, 3000 Cindel Drive, Delran, NJ 08370

Cover by Susan Eaddy
Designed by Dianna Richey

ISBN 0-86530-202-2

TABLE OF CONTENTS

About This Book

The three books in the KIDS' STUFF™ CLIP ART A LA CARTE series (fall, winter, spring) were designed to meet the many requests we have had for a collection of our unique KIDS' STUFF™ art to communicate, motivate, and appeal to students, parents, and especially to teachers. It sounds easy, but you would not believe the many hours we spent adapting and thematically organizing the hundreds of publishers quality offerings in these books. The art on each page is printed on one side only to allow for selections to be clipped and used directly from the pages or for a photo copy to be made so that the books may be kept intact for future use.

The following 101 suggestions and the illustrated projects on pages 5-7 are provided to help you get started. So we invite you to clip, snip, and enjoy KIDS' STUFF™ CLIP ART A LA CARTE. It's that easy!

Activity Cards
Art Projects
Awards
Badges
Bag Decorations
Banners
Booklet Covers
Bookmarks
Book Plates
Borders
Bracelets
Brochures
Bulletin Boards
Bulletins
Calendars
Categorization
Chalkboard
  Projects
Charts
Collages:
 •Animals
 •Ecology
 •Exercise
 •Health
 •Holidays
 •Mother Goose
 •Reading
 •Safety
 •Seasons
 •Ships and Boats
 •Toys
 •Traffic
 •Weather
Communicators

Cutups
Desk Identifiers
Dioramas
Door Knob Hangers
Envelopes
Flip-Ups
Folder Decorations
Fold-Ups
Forms
Frames
Game Boards
Game Pieces
Gift Folders
Gifts
Gift Tags
Gift Wrap Decorations
Greeting Cards
Hang-ups
Headbands
Holiday Decorations
Homework Assignments
Incentives
Invitations
Jewelry
Journals
Labels
Learning Center
  Components
Library Aids
Locker Identification
Mailboxes
Mazes
Memos
Menus

Mini Art
Mini Books
Mobiles
Motivators
Name Tags
Napkin Rings
Necklaces
Notes
Party Favors
Paste-ups
Patterns
Pick-ups
Pins
Pin-ups
Place Cards
Posters
Pop-ups
Puppets
Puzzles
Record Forms
Review Sheets
Rhyme Booklets
Room Dividers
Signs
Stand-ups
Stencils
Stick-ups
Story Starters
String-ups
Student Contracts
Student Worksheets
Teacher's Records
Tokens
Tree Decorations
Window Decorations

April 4

Nick J.

a b c d e f g
h i j k l m n o
p q r s t u v w
x y z

paper
framers
pg. 19

necklaces
pg. 75

SUE

mobiles
pg. 63

READ ME MORE STORIES

book
marks
pg. 43

borders

awards
pgs. 59 & 67

pg. 31

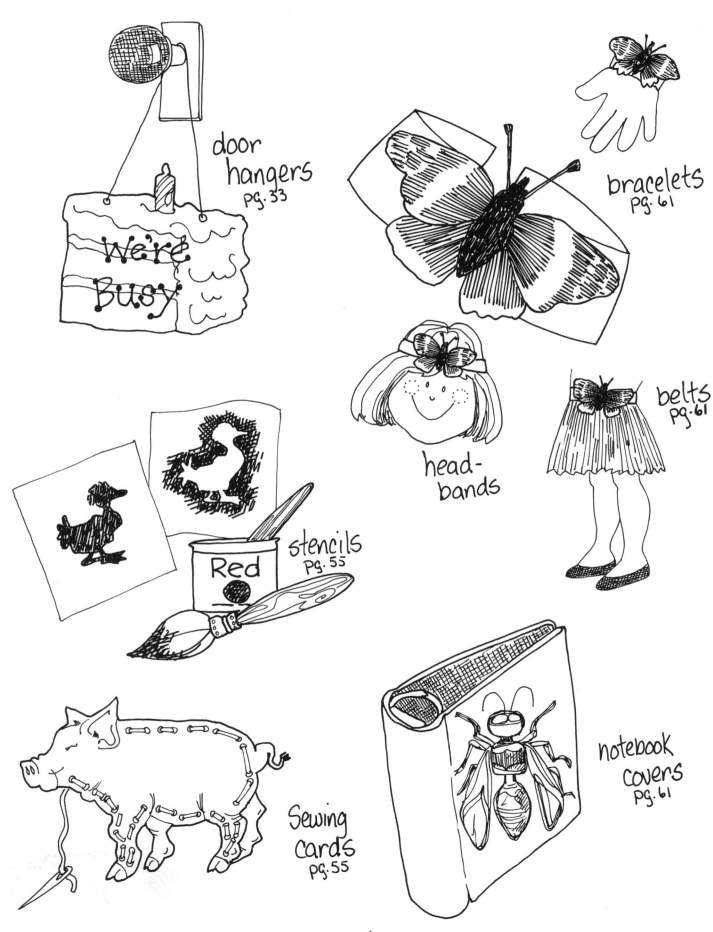

door
hangers
pg. 33

bracelets
pg. 61

We're
Busy

belts
pg. 61

head-
bands

Red

stencils
pg. 55

Sewing
cards
pg. 55

notebook
covers
pg. 61

window art pg. 23

gift tags pg. 33

TO:
FROM:

TO:
FROM:

hangers pg. 21

Posters pg. 41

Spring is Sprung

TIME:
PLACE:
R.S.V.P.

LET'S HAVE A PARTY

invitations pg. 21

SPRING

SPRING SPREE

BORDERS

HAPPY MAY DAY!

SPRING MINI ART

COMMUNICATORS AND MOTIVATORS

THOUGHT YOU'D LIKE TO KNOW!

Here's what's happening in our Classroom!

Thank You!

Hi! My name is:

HELLO! I'M ___ MY CLASS IS ON A FIELD TRIP

SPRINGING INTO SPRING WITH MOTHER GOOSE

SPECIAL DAYS

Happy Springtime

HAPPY MAY DAY!

I LOVE TO READ

Arbor Day

EARTH DAY

EASTER

BIRTHDAYS

HEALTH

WORLD

HEALTH

DAY

Take Care of Your Body!

ST. PATRICK'S DAY

Happy St. Patrick's Day

WEATHER

RAINY DAYS

RAINBOWS

UP, UP AND AWAY

ECOLOGY

Protect our natural wildlife!

DON'T LITTER!

___ is a good ecologist.

SPRING BLOSSOMS

BIRDS AND BIRDHOUSES

FISH, FROGS, AND FRIENDS

FARM FANCIES

BORDERS

PETS

WOODLAND ANIMALS

BUGS, BEES, AND BUTTERFLIES

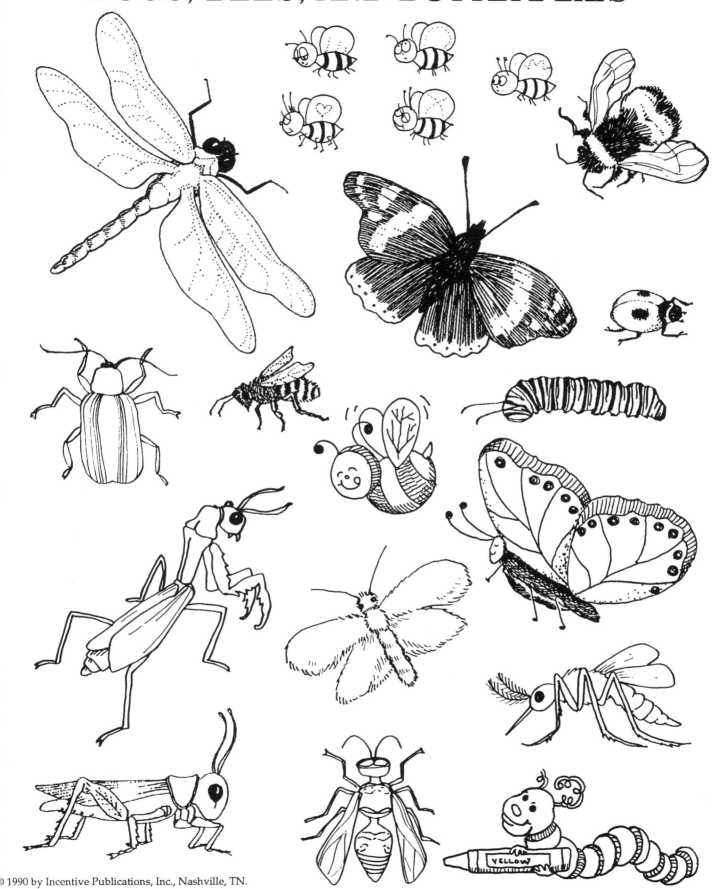

DINOSAURS

TRICERATOPS

PTERANODON

SALTOPUS

ALLOSAURUS

PROTOCERATOPS

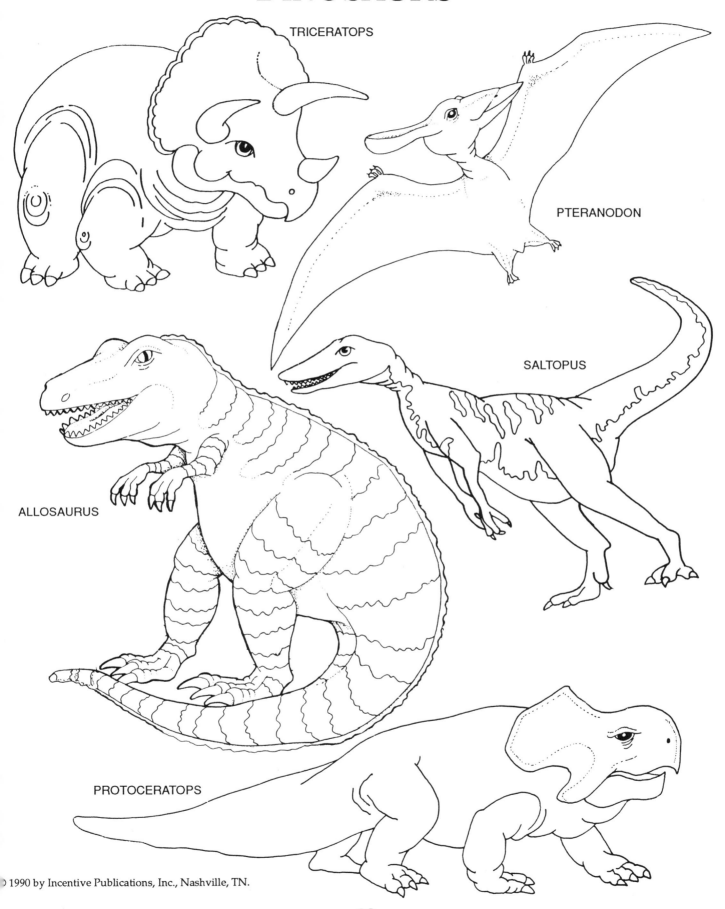

63

MERRY MUNSTERS

CUTE CRITTERS

FAMILIES AND FRIENDS

FOOD

BIG   BAR

CHOCOLATE

ON THE MOVE

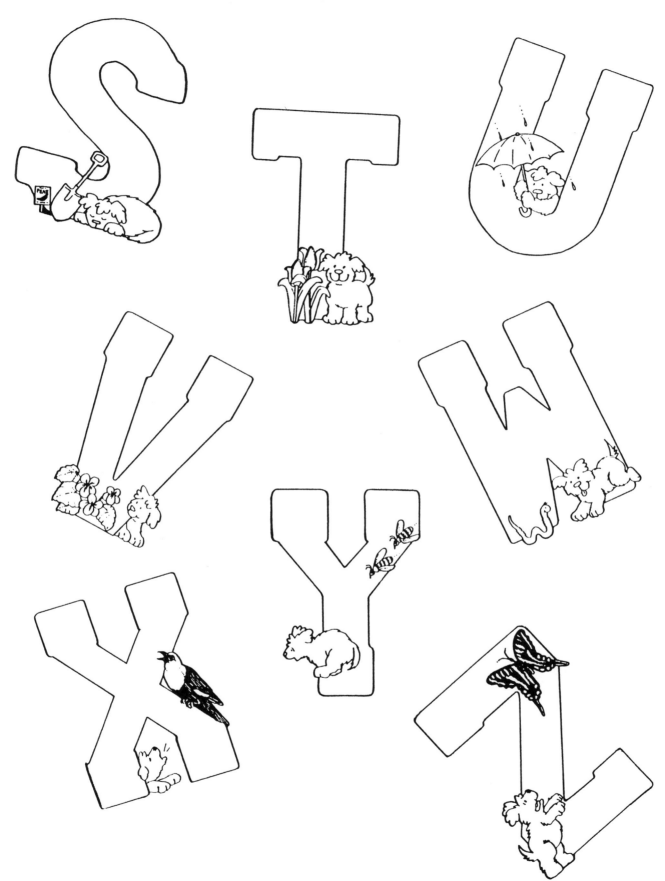